THE OFFICIAL
LIVERPOOL
FOOTBALL CLUB
ANNUAL

YOU'LL NEVER WALK ALONE

LIVERPOOL
FOOTBALL CLUB

EST. 1892

Welcome to the fourth Official Liverpool Football Club Annual from Grandreams – it's *the* book for all young Reds fans...

C000091696

CONTENTS

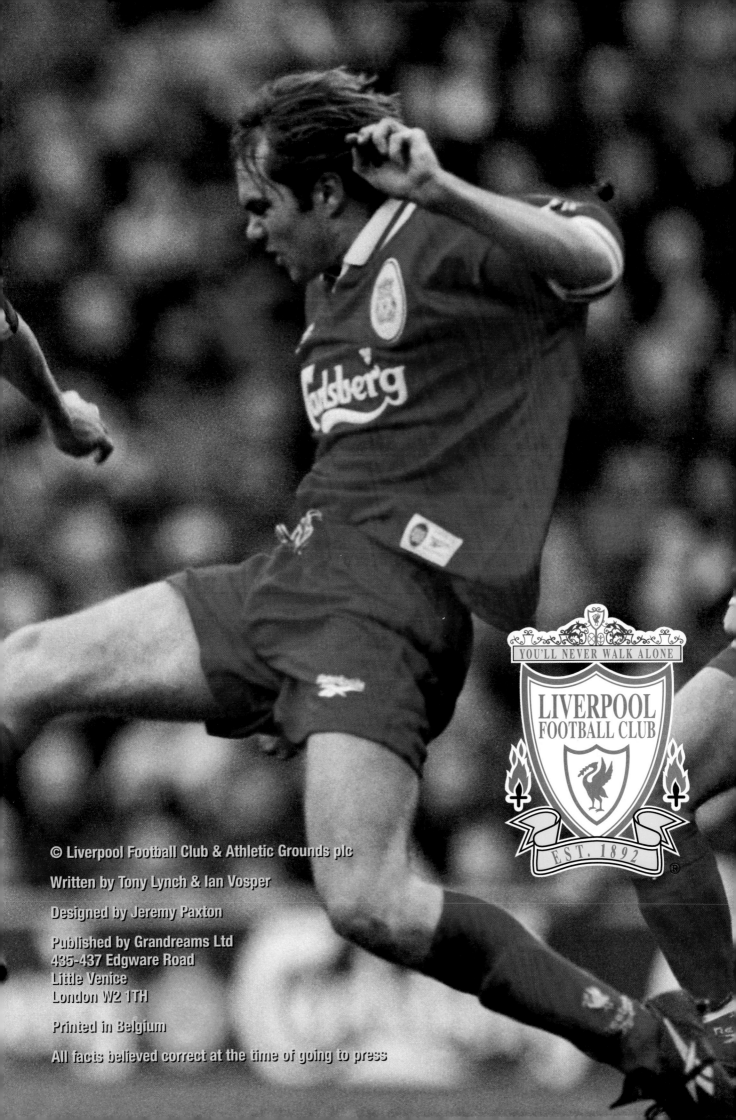

Written by Tony Lynch & Ian Vosper

Designed by Jeremy Paxton

Published by Grandreams Ltd
435-437 Edgware Road
Little Venice
London W2 1TH

Printed in Belgium

All facts believed correct at the time of going to press

LIVERPOOL FACTFILE

Roy Evans, Liverpool Team Manager

STADIUM ADDRESS
Anfield Road, Liverpool L4 OTH

TELEPHONE NUMBERS
Administration • 0151 263 2361
Match Information • 0151 260 9999 *(24 hours)*
Match Ticket Office • 0151 260 8680 *(Office hours only)*
Liverpool Superstore • 0151 263 1760
Sales & Marketing • 0151 263 9199
Public Relations • 0151 263 2361
LFC Direct Mail Order • 0990 532532
Museum & Stadium Tours • 0151 260 6677

CLUB OFFICIALS
Chairman: DR Moores
Executive Vice-Chairman: Peter B Robinson
Chief Executive: RN Parry, B.Sc, FCA
Finance Director: DMA Chestnutt, FCA
Directors: JT Cross; N White, FSCA;
TD Smith; TW Saunders; KEB Clayton, FCA
Vice-President: HE Roberts
Secretary: WB Morrison
Director of Youth: Steve Heighway

MANAGEMENT
Team Manager: Roy Evans
Assistant Manager: Doug Livermore
Coach: Ronnie Moran
Physio: Mark Leather

CLUB NICKNAME
'Pool' or 'Reds'

TEAM COLOURS
All red

THE GROUND
Current Ground Capacity: 45,362
Pitch Size: 110 x 74 yards

THE SPONSOR
Carlsberg

RED FACT
Liverpool's magnificent Roll of Honour is the most impressive of any English football club. As yet, no-one else can possibly come close to the incredible eighteen English League championships gathered by the Reds of Anfield. In fact, the earliest it could happen is in 2005, that is if Manchester United or Arsenal could win the title for the next seven seasons in a row!

& ROLL OF HONOUR...

LEAGUE CHAMPIONS – 18 TIMES
1900-01, 1905-06, 1921-22, 1922-23, 1946-47, 1963-64,
1965-66, 1972-73, 1975-76, 1976-77, 1978-79, 1979-80,
1981-82, 1982-83, 1983-84, 1985-86, 1987-88, 1989-90

League Championship Runners-up – 10 Times
1898-99, 1909-10, 1968-69, 1973-74, 1974-75, 1977-78,
1984-85, 1986-87, 1988-89, 1990-91

Second Division Champions – 4 Times
1893-94, 1895-96, 1904-05, 1961-62

FA Cup Winners – 5 Times
1965, 1974, 1986, 1989, 1992

FA Cup Runners-up – 6 Times
1914, 1950, 1971, 1977, 1988, 1996

League Cup, Milk Cup & Coca-Cola Cup Winners – 5 Times
1981, 1982, 1983, 1984, 1995

League Cup Runners-up – Twice
1978, 1987

European Cup Winners – 4 Times
1977, 1978, 1981, 1984

European Cup Runners-up – Once
1985

UEFA Cup Winners – Twice
1973, 1976

European Cup-Winners' Cup Runners-up – Once
1966

Super Cup Winners – Once
1977

World Club Championship Runners-up – Twice
1981, 1984

YOU'LL NEVER WALK ALONE

LIVERPOOL FOOTBALL CLUB

EST. 1892 ®

THE RECORDS
Record Attendance:
61,905 v Wolverhampton Wanderers,
FA Cup Fourth Round on 2.2.1952
Record League Victory:
10-1 v Rotherham Town,
Second Division on 18.2.1896
Record Defeat:
1-9 v Birmingham City,
Second Division on 11.12.1954
Record Cup Victory:
11-0 v Stromsgodset Drammen,
*European Cup-Winners' Cup First Round
first leg on 17.9.1974*
Most League Goals in a Season:
106, *Second Division in 1895-96*
Most Individual League Goals in a Season:
41, *by Roger Hunt in 1961-62*
Most League Goals in Aggregate:
245, *by Roger Hunt between 1959-1969*
Most League Appearances:
640, *by Ian Callaghan between 1960-1978*
Record Transfer Out: Stan Collymore to
Aston Villa *for £7 million*
Record Transfer In: Stan Collymore from
Nottingham Forest *for £8.5 million*

LIVERPOOL'S SQUAD NUMBERS AT THE START OF 1997-98

1 David James

2 Rob Jones

3 Bjorn Tore Kvarme

4 Jason McAteer

5 Mark Wright

6 Phil Babb

7 Steve McManaman

8 Oyvind Leonhardsen

9 Robbie Fowler

10 John Barnes

11 Jamie Redknapp

12 Steve Harkness

13 Karlheinz Riedle

14 Neil Ruddock

15 Patrik Berger

16 Michael Thomas

17 Paul Ince

18 Michael Owen

19 Mark Kennedy

20 Stig Inge Bjornebye

21 Dominic Matteo

22 Tony Warner

23 Jamie Carragher

24 Danny Murphy

25 David Thompson

26 Jorgen Nielsen

Danny Murphy in action during his Anfield debut, against Leicester

1997-98 BEGAN IN AN ATMOSPHERE of optimism and hope for the Anfield faithful. The close season had been a busy one, with the summer signing of England battler Paul Ince from Inter Milan making the biggest headlines of all. Also signing on the dotted line for Liverpool were German star Karlheinz Riedle, from European champions Borussia Dortmund, Norwegian international Oyvind Leonhardsen from Wimbledon, and Danny Murphy, an impressive young midfielder from Crewe Alexandra.

After pre-season games in Sweden, Denmark, Ireland and Norway, and friendly matches against Bristol City and Crewe Alexandra, manager Roy Evans declared that his 'jigsaw' was just about complete, especially with the capture of Paul Ince. He also spoke of the high expectations among the fans and players of Liverpool FC. "We know that winning is all that matters this season and I'm confident that we have the squad to achieve the success we all crave," he said. Only time would tell.

1997-98 part one

Steve Harkness is challenged by Leeds United's Jimmy Floyd Hasselbaink

Karlheinz Riedle moves away from Wimbledon's Vinnie Jones

AUGUST 1997

The Reds' opening match of the season was played in a virtual heat wave at **WIMBLEDON's** *Selhurst Park* on 9 August. New acquisition Paul Ince was appointed club captain shortly before this match. It was also to be John Barnes' last match for Liverpool – he was an unused sub in the contest. A few days later John moved on a free transfer to Newcastle United (where he would be reunited with former Anfield heroes Kenny Dalglish and Ian Rush).

The Dons opened the scoring through Marcus Gayle in the 56th minute, but Liverpool levelled the scoreline when young Michael Owen scored from the penalty-spot in the 72nd minute after Vinny Jones had brought down Karlheinz Riedle.

Liverpool's first home match of the season brought **LEICESTER CITY** to Anfield. It proved to be a poor performance by the Reds who went down 2-1. City's first goal stunned Anfield, as it came after just 74 seconds. Some sloppy Liverpool defending contributed to Leicester's second in the 83rd minute, scored by Matt Elliott. The bright point in the match came when Paul Ince scored his first goal for the Reds on 84 minutes – a glorious strike from all of 25 yards.

A visit to **BLACKBURN ROVERS** followed on 23 August. Michael Owen was the star for Liverpool and he opened the scoring with a magnificent, calmly taken, solo goal on

RED FACT

The game against Leicester City on 13 August 1997 marked Liverpool's first opening home-match defeat in 32 years!

THE REDS IN 1997-98

The Reds celebrate Michael Owen's equaliser against the Dons

52 minutes. The Reds appeared to be heading for their first three-pointer of the season, but it wasn't to be. With just six minutes left to play, Rovers' sub Martin Dahlin hit the equaliser and the points were shared.

Three days later Liverpool travelled to *Elland Road*, to take on **LEEDS UNITED**. And this time the Reds did come home with all three points in the bag. Steve McManaman got the first goal in a torrid first half that saw loads of action from 'keeper David James as United peppered his goal with shots. The Liverpool goal came under regular bombardment in the second half too, but again David was

in tip-top form and managed to keep them all out. The other highlight of the match came in the 74th minute when Karlheinz Riedle scored his first goal in English football. Spotting Leeds' 'keeper Nigel Martyn off his line, the German international chipped the ball right into the top corner of his net. The victory lifted Liverpool eight places up the Premiership table, from 16th to 8th.

MATCH FAX

RESULT	COMPETITION	DATE	STADIUM	ATTENDANCE
Wimbledon 1, Liverpool 1	Premiership	9.8.97	Selhurst Park	26,106
Liverpool 1, Leicester 2	Premiership	13.8.97	Anfield	35,007
Blackburn 1, Liverpool 1	Premiership	23.8.97	Ewood Park	30,187
Leeds 0, Liverpool 2	Premiership	26.8.97	Elland Road	39,775

August '97

Michael Owen scores for Liverpool against Blackburn

Paul Ince tackles Neal Ardley

10

Paul Ince opens the scoring against Sheffield Wednesday

SEPTEMBER 1997

SHEFFIELD WEDNESDAY came to Anfield on 13 September. This time midfield aces Michael Thomas and Paul Ince were the heroes of the hour. Paul scored the opening goal on 55 minutes after Wednesday's defence had seemed impenetrable. Twelve minutes later Michael put 'Pool two-up. After that Wednesday pressed forward and were rewarded with a goal in the closing minutes from Paulo Di Canio. But it wasn't enough – **Liverpool** had three more points in the bag.

Liverpool's European adventure began in Glasgow on 16 September, when the club took on **CELTIC** in the 1st Round 1st Leg of the UEFA Cup. A crowd of almost 49,000 packed *Parkhead* for what promised to be a classic 'Battle of Britain' encounter. Young Michael Owen was making his European competition debut in this match, yet you'd be forgiven for thinking he was an experienced old hand. After just six minutes Michael produced a goal of stunning quality. Receiving a Karlheinz Riedle pass, he then eluded defender Alan Stubbs and 'keeper Jonathan Gould to chip the ball into the net.

After that moment of near genius from **Liverpool**, Celtic got their act together. Shortly after the start of the second period they drew level through Jackie McNamara. Then, with around 18 minutes left to play, the Scots went ahead through a spot-kick after David James was adjudged to have fouled Henrik Larsson. Enter Steve McManaman to save the day – shortly after that Celtic strike, SuperMac collected the ball inside the **Liverpool** half. He then proceeded to jink his way forward, past player after player, on a 70-yard run that resulted in a terrific goal. **Liverpool** had equalised and the away goals would offer a good deal of protection in the return leg.

It was back to Premiership action on 20 September and a visit to **SOUTHAMPTON** where the points were shared in a 1-1 draw. Karlheinz Riedle opened the scoring in the

Paul Ince and Rob Jones shadow Wednesday's Paulo Di Canio

37th minute with a powerful close range header. The Saints replied just after half time through Kevin Davies. Once again David James was in great form, pulling off a terrific save from Davies late in the game. Robbie Fowler, who came on as a sub for his first appearance of the season, almost pulled off a winner.

The next game at Anfield, on 22 September, was arguably **Liverpool**'s best performance of the season so far. **ASTON VILLA** were the victims in an inspired second half display by the Reds. Robbie Fowler, making his first start of the season after five months out through injury, got the ball rolling with a penalty after Gareth Southgate had fouled Michael Owen. Then Steve McManaman took charge to score another superb individual goal. This time Macca only had to run a mere 50 yards with the ball, before unleashing a shot that beat Mark Bosnich in the Villa goal. The job was

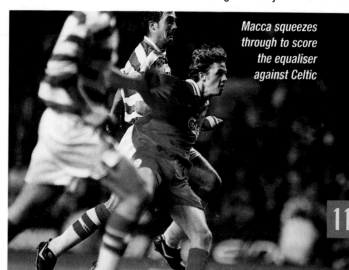

Macca squeezes through to score the equaliser against Celtic

THE REDS IN 1997-98

Karlheinz Riedle in action against Southampton

completed with a Karlheinz Riedle goal in the last minute, after a brilliant solo run by Michael Owen.

This match marked an unhappy return to Anfield for Stan Collymore. It was his first trip to **Liverpool** since his £7 million move to Villa just a few weeks earlier.

The next Premiership outing brought **Liverpool** right back down to earth. The visit to **WEST HAM UNITED** on 27 September was a tough one. The Hammers went ahead through John Hartson on 14 minutes, then, back to form Robbie Fowler volleyed a second half equaliser. But West Ham ran out as winners after Eyal Berkovic pounced on a loose ball and fired it past David James in the 64th minute.

The wonder goal scored by Steve McManaman to equalise against **CELTIC** in the UEFA Cup two weeks earlier, proved absolutely invaluable in the return leg at Anfield on 30 September. Celtic were relentless in attack, especially in the first hour of the match – and only a spirited display by the **Liverpool** defence kept them out. Phil Babb was particularly effective. Celtic could not break

down the barricades. The match ended in a 0-0 scoreline and the tie in a 2-2 aggregate. **Liverpool** were through to the 2nd Round on away goals.

RED FACT
Robbie Fowler's penalty success on 22 September 1997 was his eleventh goal in just ten matches against Aston Villa!

Getting shirty – West Ham's John Hartson and Liverpool's Jamie Carragher

MATCH FAX

RESULT	COMPETITION	DATE	STADIUM	ATTENDANCE
Liverpool 2, Sheffield Wed 1	Premiership	13.9.97	Anfield	34,705
Celtic 2, Liverpool 2	UEFA Cup (1)	16.9.97	Parkhead	48,526
Southampton 1, Liverpool 1	Premiership	20.9.97	The Dell	15,252
Liverpool 3, Aston Villa 0	Premiership	22.9.97	Anfield	34,843
West Ham 2, Liverpool 1	Premiership	27.9.97	Upton Park	25,908
Liverpool 0, Celtic 0	UEFA Cup (1)	30.9.97	Anfield	38,205

September '97

THE REDS IN 1997-98

OCTOBER 1997

Ruud Gullit's flamboyant **CHELSEA** were the first visitors to Anfield in October. The Blues had started their season well and were definitely up among the serious challengers for the title. They were currently lying in 4th position, while Liverpool were 9th.

Liverpool's Czech Republic international, Patrik Berger, repeated his previous season's performance in this fixture, by becoming Man of the Match. In fact, he went one better in '97 by notching a superb hat-trick – he had scored twice in 1996 when Liverpool won 5-1.

Patrik opened the scoring in the 20th minute when he lobbed Chelsea 'keeper Ed de Goey after Graeme Le Saux had fumbled a clearance. Gianfranco Zola equalised for the Blues two minutes later, although Bjorn Kvarme had been bundled out of the action in a collision with Mark Hughes and the Reds felt they were hard done by.

Berger put Liverpool back in front on 35 minutes by firing home from a Stig Bjornebye cross. The hat-trick was completed in the 57th minute when Patrik beat Chelsea's offside trap before drilling the ball home. Seven minutes

Above: Steve McManaman breaks through the Chelsea defence

Below: Patrik Berger scores Liverpool's second against Chelsea

later Berger was the provider as Robbie Fowler made it 4-1. Chelsea's consolation came in the 85th minute when Gustavo Poyet scored from the spot to settle the scoreline at 4-2.

Next came **Liverpool**'s first Coca-Cola Cup outing of the season – an away 3rd Round tie at **WEST BROMWICH ALBION** on 15 October. Patrik Berger and Robbie Fowler kept up their scoring form by notching a goal each in the Reds' 2-0 victory.

The first Merseyside derby of the campaign took place three days later at **EVERTON**'s *Goodison Park*. The Blues had had a shaky start to the season and were already dipping a toe in the murky waters of the relegation zone.

Right: Macca has just missed against Strasbourg but (below) he's on target against Derby

	RESULT	COMPETITION	DATE	STADIUM	ATTENDANCE	
MATCH FAX	Liverpool 4, Chelsea 2	Premiership	5.10.97	Anfield	36,647	**October '97**
	West Brom 0, Liverpool 2	Coca-Cola Cup (3)	15.10.97	The Hawthorns	21,986	
	Everton 2, Liverpool 0	Premiership	18.10.97	Goodison Park	40,112	
	Strasbourg 3, Liverpool 0	UEFA Cup (2)	21.10.97	de la Meinau	18,813	
	Liverpool 4, Derby 0	Premiership	25.10.97	Anfield	38,017	

Everton's Dave Watson and Liverpool's Robbie Fowler can't quite see the ball in the Goodison sunshine!

But on this occasion – buoyed up by local pride – they pulled out all the stops to record a 2-0 victory. An unfortunate own-goal by Neil Ruddock gave the Blues the lead just before half time. Fifteen minutes from the end, Everton prodigy Danny Cadamarteri dispossessed Bjorn Kvarme and ran on to score.

RACING CLUB DE STRASBOURG were Liverpool's opponents in the UEFA Cup 2nd Round. The 1st leg was played in France on 21 October. Two goals from David Zitelli and one from Denni Conteh, without reply, virtually put the tie beyond the Reds' reach. Robbie Fowler came close to pulling one back with a great lob, but 'keeper Alexander Vencel just managed to tip the ball over the bar.

Four days later **DERBY COUNTY** came up against Liverpool's reaction to that Euro defeat. In complete contrast to the dire display in France, this Premiership encounter at Anfield saw a rampant Reds performance.

Oyvind Leonhardsen is challenged by Derby's Mauricio Solis

It proved to be a red letter day for Robbie Fowler, who scored twice in the 4-0 victory. Oyvind Leonhardsen was delighted too, as he scored his first goal in a Liverpool shirt, having only recently made it into the first team due to a hamstring injury picked up in a pre-season friendly.

Man of the Match, however, was livewire Steve McManaman, who ran things from midfield and contributed the fourth goal from a rocket header. The result took the Reds into 5th position, their highest Premiership placing of the season to date.

NOVEMBER 1997

November looked to be a promising month for the Reds, especially with four home games on the trot. First, though, came a Premiership visit on 1 November, to **BOLTON WANDERERS'** magnificent *Reebok Stadium*. Robbie Fowler scored in the first minute when he put away an Oyvind Leonhardsen pass. Liverpool remained the dominant side, keeping possession as Bolton seemed to flounder. But then, in the 75th minute, Robbie over-reacted to the close attention he had been receiving all afternoon and referee Gallagher had no hesitation in issuing his marching orders. Bolton boss Colin Todd re-grouped to take advantage of the situation – and a Nathan Blake goal on 84 minutes earned Wanderers a share of the points.

On 4 November **STRASBOURG** came to Anfield for the UEFA Cup 2nd Round 2nd Leg – and with that 3-0 lead to

Hot Shot Robbie Fowler scores against Bolton

protect. And that's just what they did throughout the first half as the Reds pressed forward constantly in search of a breakthrough. But at half time the scoreline remained stuck at 0-0. It was a different story in the second period. Roy Evans sacrificed two defenders, Rob Jones and Stig Bjornebye, in favour of known goal-getters Karlheinz Riedle and Patrik Berger.

In the 62nd minute Karlheinz was tripped in the area. Robbie Fowler stepped up and claimed his eighth goal in eleven appearances. With six minutes left, Riedle showed his class by heading home **Liverpool**'s second goal of the evening. But it wasn't enough. Despite the Reds' 2-0 victory, Strasbourg went through with a 3-2 aggregate. **Liverpool**'s Euro ambitions would have to be put on ice once more. Now the club would have to ensure continental qualification again for the 1998-99 season.

Liverpool were back in Premiership action on 8 November when **TOTTENHAM HOTSPUR** came to Anfield.

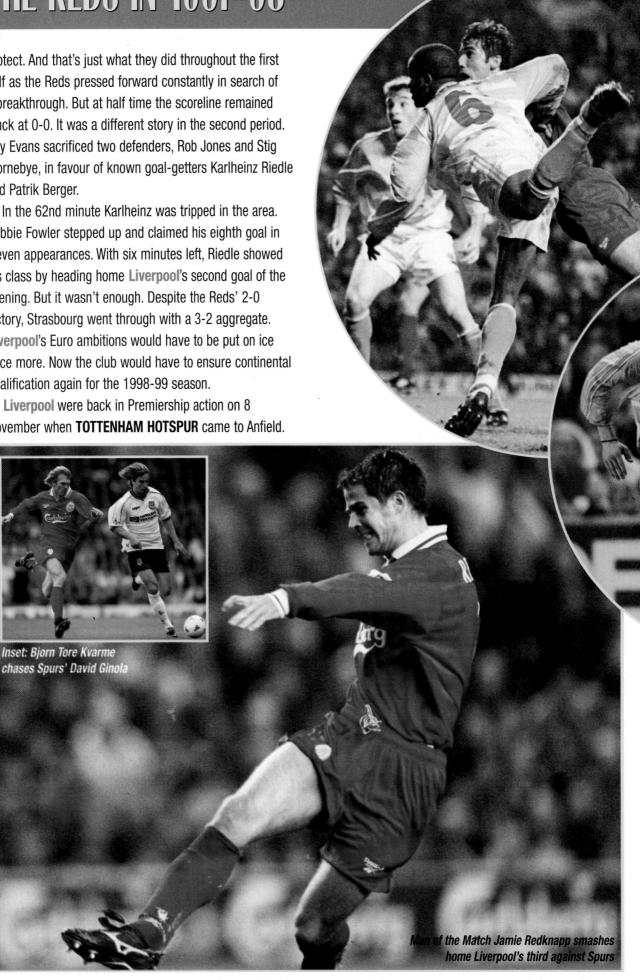

Inset: Bjorn Tore Kvarme chases Spurs' David Ginola

Man of the Match Jamie Redknapp smashes home Liverpool's third against Spurs

Top: Riedle makes it 2-0 against Strasbourg
Middle: Bjorn Tore Kvarme evades a tackle in the European encounter against Strasbourg
Bottom: Karlheinz Riedle goes flying in the match versus Barnsley

Celebrations after Macca's goal at Highbury!

Spurs were experiencing a torrid time in their Premiership campaign. They had yet to win away from home and were languishing in 15th place in the table. The Reds did them no favours. If anything, the final scoreline underlined the extent of the problems facing the North London outfit.

The first half was evenly balanced and the sides went in for the interval at 0-0. Then, three minutes into the second period, Spurs 'keeper Ian Walker failed to hold onto a Jamie Redknapp shot. He dropped the ball into the path of Steve McManaman, who said 'thanks a lot' and hit it home from two yards out.

Oyvind Leonhardsen was the next name on the score sheet when he fired home in the 50th minute. Next, Man of the Match Jamie Redknapp scored a cracker from 25 yards. Substitute Michael Owen rounded off the rout when he caught up with a Paul Ince pass that should have been easily collected by Walker. But Michael got there first and placed the ball in the empty net – this was Michael's first ever first team goal in front of the Anfield faithful.

Ten days later Michael took his Anfield tally to four goals and notched his first hat-trick for the club. The team on the receiving end was Second Division **GRIMSBY TOWN** who came to Anfield on 18 November for the 4th Round of the Coca-Cola Cup. The first Owen goal was a relatively easy tap-in after he had followed up on a Jamie Redknapp shot that Grimsby 'keeper Aiden Davison could not hold. The second came from the penalty-spot after Michael had been upended by defender Peter Handyside. The third was a striker's delight. Owen collected a superb pass from Steve McManaman on the edge of the box, glanced up and aimed for the top corner of the Mariners' net. **Liverpool** went through to the 5th Round in devastating style.

There was no such satisfying result on the following Saturday, when the Premiership's bottom club, **BARNSLEY**,

came to Anfield – and went home with all three points. Despite being on top for most of the game, the **Liverpool** forwards failed to breach the Barnsley defence. The visitors scored in the 35th minute when Ashley Ward took advantage of a defensive blunder by Patrik Berger. The result lifted Barnsley off the foot of the table and nudged **Liverpool** down from 6th to 8th.

November closed with **Liverpool**'s visit to championship challengers **ARSENAL** who were so far unbeaten in the League at *Highbury*. The Reds, playing in their vivid yellow away strip, were about to put an end to that impressive statistic. The match was settled by a single goal, scored by **Liverpool**'s resident midfield genius, and Man of the Match, Steve McManaman. The goal came in the 56th minute when Macca collected a Bjorn Kvarme throw-in, took the ball to the edge of the area and unleashed a volley which took David Seaman completely by surprise.

It was a great victory that restored **Liverpool**'s title hopes and put the side in good spirits for the forthcoming visit to Anfield by the reigning champions.

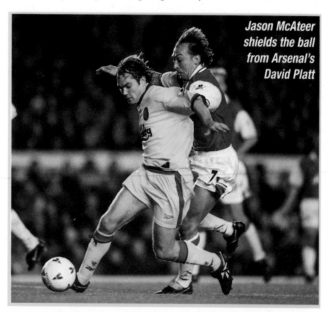

Jason McAteer shields the ball from Arsenal's David Platt

	RESULT	COMPETITION	DATE	STADIUM	ATTENDANCE	
MATCH FAX	Bolton 1, Liverpool 1	Premiership	1.11.97	Reebok Stadium	25,000	**November '97**
	Liverpool 2, Strasbourg 0	UEFA Cup (2)	4.11.97	Anfield	32,426	
	Liverpool 4, Tottenham 0	Premiership	8.11.97	Anfield	38,006	
	Liverpool 3, Grimsby 0	Coca-Cola Cup (4)	18.11.97	Anfield	28,515	
	Liverpool 0, Barnsley 1	Premiership	22.11.97	Anfield	41,011	
	Arsenal 0, Liverpool 1	Premiership	30.11.97	Highbury	38,094	

Manchester United's Andy Cole makes a crash landing while Dominic Matteo remains airborne

DECEMBER 1997

MANCHESTER UNITED were sitting on top of the table on 6 December and **Liverpool** were hoping to topple them from that lofty position, and to avenge the 3-1 defeat in the previous season's corresponding fixture. Alas, it wasn't to be. The scoreline was stuck at 0-0 after a full-blooded first half. But six minutes into the second period, United went ahead through Andy Cole who capitalised on a mistake by Bjorn Kvarme.

Nine minutes later Michael Owen was felled in the box and, despite United's protestations to referee Elleray, the spot kick was awarded. Sure shot Robbie Fowler made no mistake in equalising. After that, Alex Ferguson's side took charge and eventually finished as 3-1 winners (again!), thanks to further goals from David Beckham and Andy Cole. The Anfield faithful were disappointed by their side's poor performance which resulted in a slip back to 8th place in the table – and put a big dent in those title aspirations.

Next up was a trip to South London on 13 December for the Premiership fixture with relegation-threatened **CRYSTAL PALACE** – a club who were finding it difficult to win at home. **Liverpool** did nothing to alter that situation and emerged as comfortable 3-0 victors. The goals came

INSET: Oyvind Leonhardsen reaches the ball ahead of United's Phil Neville

Robbie puts a penalty past Peter Schmeichel

19

from Steve McManaman, Michael Owen and Oyvind Leonhardsen. Man of the Match was Michael Owen, who put in an all-round stunning performance.

A single goal settled the next match in Liverpool's favour. **COVENTRY CITY** were the Anfield visitors five days before Christmas. Once again Michael Owen, just six days past his 18th birthday, was Liverpool's hero. In the 14th minute he scored by putting the finishing touch to a great build up by Jamie Redknapp and Steve McManaman. Liverpool and Coventry were due to meet again in the New Year when they would contest an FA Cup 3rd Round tie.

Liverpool's last home fixture of 1997 brought **LEEDS UNITED** to Anfield. Under George Graham's leadership Leeds were enjoying a productive season. Before the kick-off they were three points ahead of the Reds in the Premiership table. By the end of 90 minutes that gap had been closed. Wonderkid Michael Owen scored the opening goal early in the second half after Oyvind Leonhardsen had set him up. Then Robbie Fowler took over the scoring duties bagging two goals, before Leeds could claw one back through Alf Inge Haaland.

The Reds closed the first half of the 1997-98 campaign in the most satisfying style, with a cracking 2-1 victory against Kenny Dalglish's **NEWCASTLE UNITED** at *St James' Park*. Steve Howey had given the Magpies an early lead, but that was wiped out by Steve McManaman's first goal, a stunning 20-yard right-foot volley that gave Shaka Hislop no chance. Macca's winner also came from that trusty right boot when he latched onto a great pass from Michael Owen shortly before half time.

Four Premiership victories in a row had taken Liverpool to 4th place in the table. Next the Reds would turn their attention to the world's most famous Cup competition, the FA Cup.

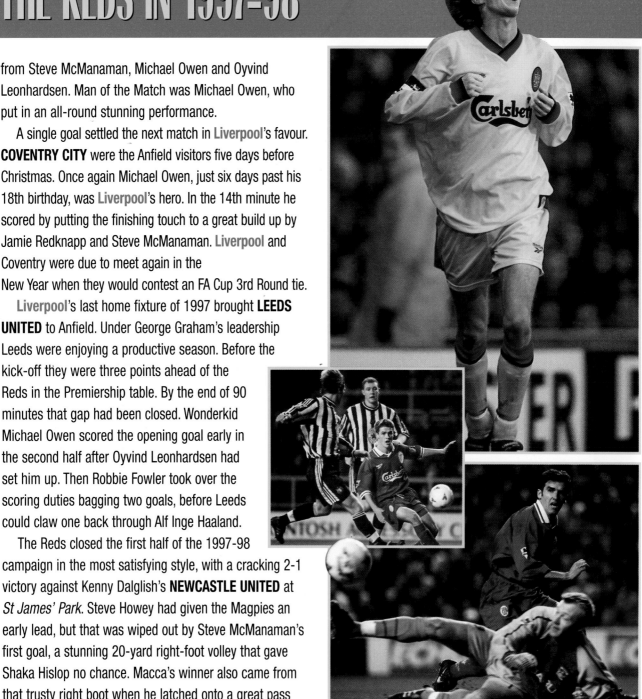

Top: Macca is overjoyed after scoring against Crystal Palace
Middle: Newcastle's Warren Barton and Steve Watson keep an eye on Liverpool's wonderkid, Michael Owen
Bottom: Goalmouth action in Liverpool's victory over Leeds

LIVERPOOL IN 1997-98 CONTINUES ON PAGE 50

MATCH FAX

RESULT	COMPETITION	DATE	STADIUM	ATTENDANCE
Liverpool 1, Man United 3	Premiership	6.12.97	Anfield	41,027
Crystal Palace 0, Liverpool 3	Premiership	13.12.97	Selhurst Park	25,790
Liverpool 1, Coventry City 0	Premiership	20.12.97	Anfield	39,707
Liverpool 3, Leeds United 1	Premiership	26.12.97	Anfield	43,854
Newcastle United 1, Liverpool 2	Premiership	28.12.97	St. James' Park	36,702

December '97

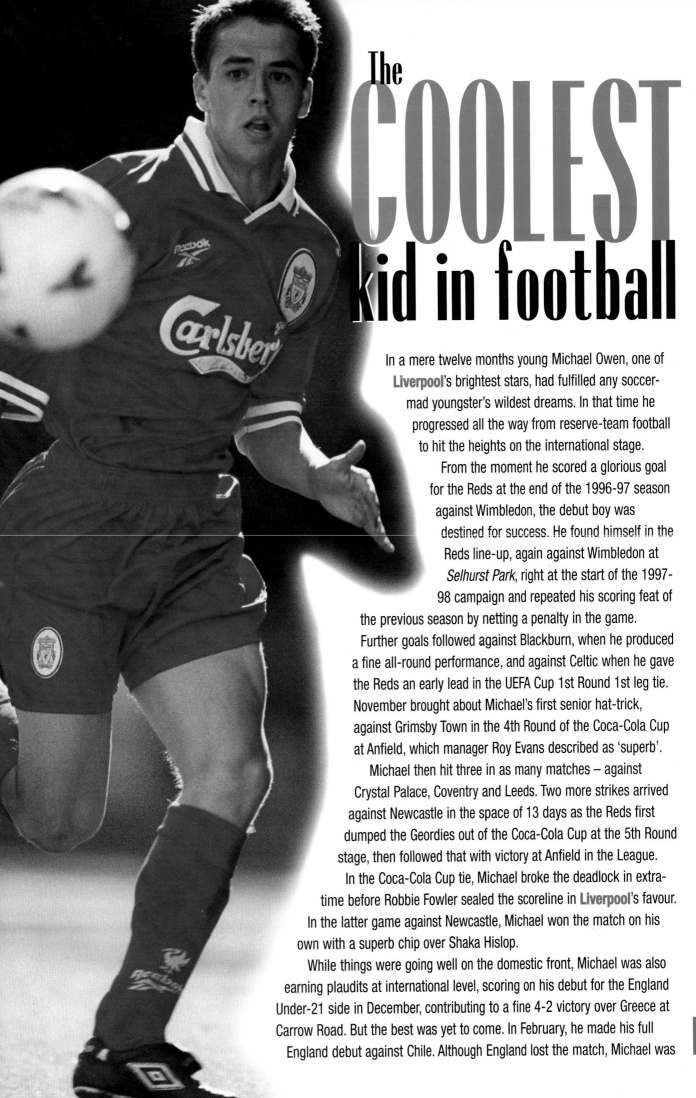

The COOLEST kid in football

In a mere twelve months young Michael Owen, one of Liverpool's brightest stars, had fulfilled any soccer-mad youngster's wildest dreams. In that time he progressed all the way from reserve-team football to hit the heights on the international stage.

From the moment he scored a glorious goal for the Reds at the end of the 1996-97 season against Wimbledon, the debut boy was destined for success. He found himself in the Reds line-up, again against Wimbledon at *Selhurst Park*, right at the start of the 1997-98 campaign and repeated his scoring feat of the previous season by netting a penalty in the game.

Further goals followed against Blackburn, when he produced a fine all-round performance, and against Celtic when he gave the Reds an early lead in the UEFA Cup 1st Round 1st leg tie. November brought about Michael's first senior hat-trick, against Grimsby Town in the 4th Round of the Coca-Cola Cup at Anfield, which manager Roy Evans described as 'superb'.

Michael then hit three in as many matches – against Crystal Palace, Coventry and Leeds. Two more strikes arrived against Newcastle in the space of 13 days as the Reds first dumped the Geordies out of the Coca-Cola Cup at the 5th Round stage, then followed that with victory at Anfield in the League.

In the Coca-Cola Cup tie, Michael broke the deadlock in extra-time before Robbie Fowler sealed the scoreline in Liverpool's favour. In the latter game against Newcastle, Michael won the match on his own with a superb chip over Shaka Hislop.

While things were going well on the domestic front, Michael was also earning plaudits at international level, scoring on his debut for the England Under-21 side in December, contributing to a fine 4-2 victory over Greece at Carrow Road. But the best was yet to come. In February, he made his full England debut against Chile. Although England lost the match, Michael was

21

The COOLEST kid in football

The raised finger means yet another goal!

very impressive and he walked off with a well-deserved Man of the Match award.

At 18 years and 59 days he became the youngest player this Century to represent England. Said Roy Evans: "Michael was fantastic and didn't look at all out of place. He was dangerous whenever he had the ball and his pace was evident on a number of occasions."

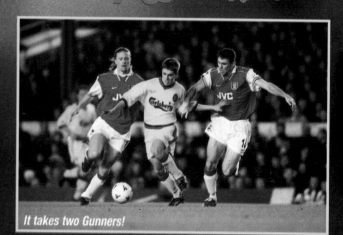

It takes two Gunners!

England team boss Glenn Hoddle has been just as glowing in his praise, mentioning the qualities that Michael possesses in the same breath as those of Brazilian star Ronaldo. Either side of the England game, Michael gave five-star showings against Southampton and Sheffield Wednesday. The Saints' victory took some gloss off the proceedings from a **Liverpool** point of view, but the youngster scored twice in the surprise 3-2 reversal.

Only three days after that historic international against Chile, he hit the most superb hat-trick in sublime fashion at Hillsborough. With the Reds 3-1 down and seemingly heading for defeat, the 18-year-old struck in devastating fashion, with two late stunners.

Naturally, Roy Evans was absolutely delighted: "I think he upstaged what he did against Chile," said the **Liverpool** manager. "You can see what he is capable of. He got three and may have had a couple more. It was a fantastic performance."

On the subject of goal scoring, Michael finished the 1997-98 campaign with 23 goals, a superb achievement to add to three international caps in his first full season.

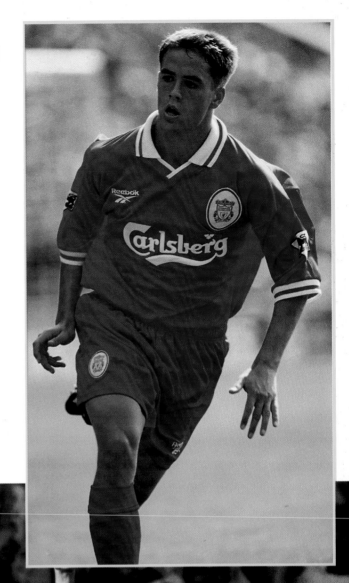

Celebration time for Liverpool's latest goal machine...and the fans!

PLAYER FACT FILE
YOU'LL NEVER WALK ALONE
MICHAEL JAMES OWEN
Birthdate: 14 December 1979
Birthplace: Chester
Height: 5' 9"
Weight: 10st 4lb
Previous clubs: None
International Honours:
England Schools, Youth & Full

KEEPING

A close look at Liverpool's two international goalkeepers

After what must have seemed like an eternity for the big American international, Brad Friedel finally signed for the Reds from the United States club **COLOMBUS CREW** in December 1997. **Liverpool** had been interested in signing Brad since the early 1990s, but he was refused a work permit by the Department of Employment due to his lack of international caps. However, once he began to make appearances for the United States on a regular basis, he was hopeful that a move to **Liverpool** would finally come his way. Brad takes up the story: "The club stood by me when the decision went against us, so I was prepared to wait in order to get a move to Anfield."

In fact, he had several opportunities to sign for top European sides when his original application for a work permit at Anfield was rejected, but he had set his heart on **Liverpool**. He continues: "I have always wanted to play at the top level in professional football and you cannot get much further up the ladder than by playing for **Liverpool**'s first team."

Yet, even after Brad had signed, he had to wait until the last day in February to finally make his full debut. Following eleven appearances on the bench, he had his first outing at Aston Villa. The following week he made his home debut against Bolton Wanderers and called it 'a great experience'. There are bound to be many more great experiences for Brad as he guards the goal for **Liverpool**.

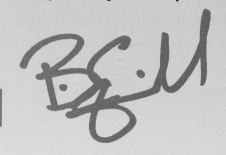

PLAYER FACT FILE
YOU'LL NEVER WALK ALONE

BRAD FRIEDEL

Birthdate: 18 May 1971

Birthplace: USA

Previous club:

Columbus Crew

International Honours:

USA Full

'EM OUT

David gathers the ball safely in local derby action against Everton

David James is a former England Under-21 international who won ten intermediate caps while with his previous club, **WATFORD**, from whom he signed in June 1992 for £1,000,000. In March 1997 he made his full international debut in England's 2-0 victory over Mexico at Wembley, in which his **Liverpool** team-mate Robbie Fowler scored the second goal. Not surprisingly, David was delighted to keep a clean sheet. "It gave me a great deal of personal pride, although there wasn't a lot to do – I think they only had one shot on target," he said. But following that elevation to full international status last year, the big 'keeper hasn't been called upon again and there's no doubting the sense of disappointment he feels. "It's hard to think that I played for England at Wembley last year and haven't been involved since."

The 1997-98 League season saw mixed fortunes for David, who began the campaign as **Liverpool**'s first choice and was particularly inspired in the 2-0 victory at Leeds United. But when Brad Freidel signed for the club last December, James' previously automatic place was in jeopardy. He finally gave way to Brad in February at Aston Villa after he had started in every one of the previous 37 first team matches. Thereafter, David had to be content with a place on the bench as the season drew to a close.

25

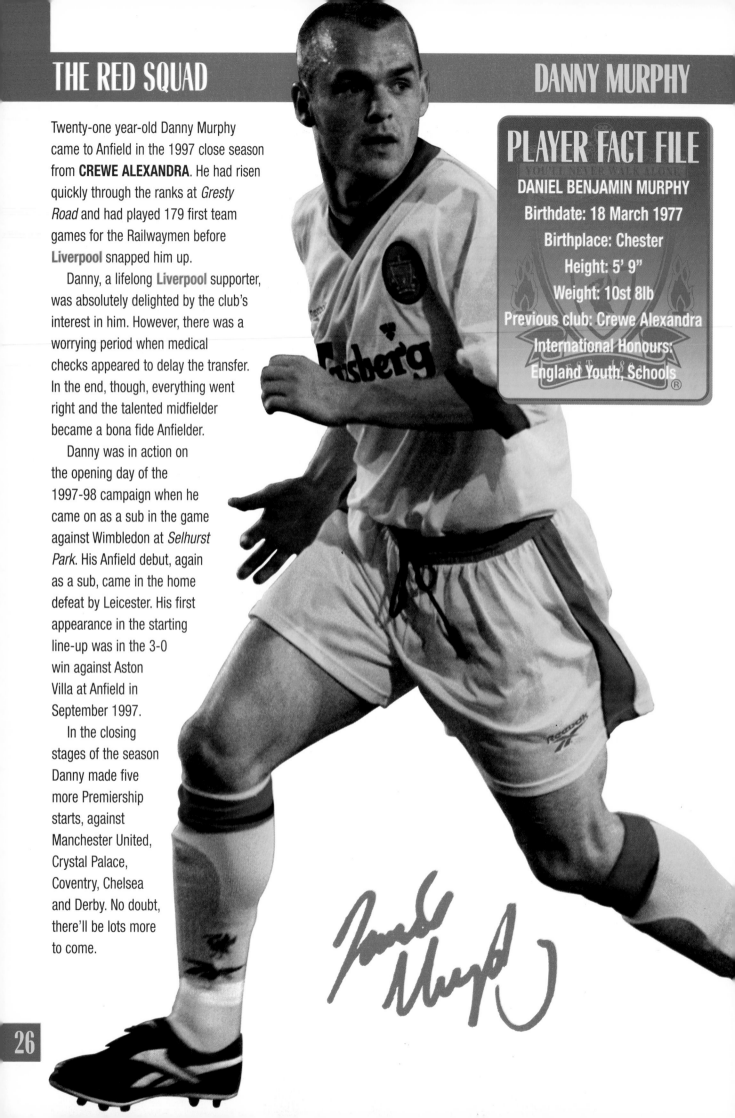

Twenty-one year-old Danny Murphy came to Anfield in the 1997 close season from **CREWE ALEXANDRA**. He had risen quickly through the ranks at *Gresty Road* and had played 179 first team games for the Railwaymen before **Liverpool** snapped him up.

Danny, a lifelong **Liverpool** supporter, was absolutely delighted by the club's interest in him. However, there was a worrying period when medical checks appeared to delay the transfer. In the end, though, everything went right and the talented midfielder became a bona fide Anfielder.

Danny was in action on the opening day of the 1997-98 campaign when he came on as a sub in the game against Wimbledon at *Selhurst Park*. His Anfield debut, again as a sub, came in the home defeat by Leicester. His first appearance in the starting line-up was in the 3-0 win against Aston Villa at Anfield in September 1997.

In the closing stages of the season Danny made five more Premiership starts, against Manchester United, Crystal Palace, Coventry, Chelsea and Derby. No doubt, there'll be lots more to come.

PLAYER FACT FILE

YOU'LL NEVER WALK ALONE

DANIEL BENJAMIN MURPHY
Birthdate: 18 March 1977
Birthplace: Chester
Height: 5' 9"
Weight: 10st 8lb
Previous club: Crewe Alexandra
International Honours:
England Youth, Schools

26

The grandson of Billy Jones who played for the Reds in the 1950 FA Cup final against Arsenal, Rob is one of **Liverpool**'s most consistent performers. He made a welcome return to the **Liverpool** first team at the beginning of the 1997-98 season following a miserable time in the previous campaign, when he was only able to make two Premiership appearances, due to injury.

Rob was signed for a bargain £300,000 from **CREWE ALEXANDRA** in October 1991 and, following impressive performances, he made his full England debut in the 2-0 victory over France at Wembley in February 1992, ironically even before his baptism at Under-21 level.

Three months later, in May 1992, he won an FA Cup Winners' medal as **Liverpool** beat Sunderland 2-0 at Wembley. In the 1997-98 season Rob was back to his best form until an Achilles tendon injury struck in November, and he had to wait until late January for his return when he came off the bench against Blackburn.

But for injury, Rob would surely have passed the 200 League appearances mark for the Reds by now. At just 26 years of age he harbours hopes of a return to the international stage and will want to add to his eight full caps as England attempt to qualify for the European Championships in 2000.

PLAYER FACT FILE
YOU'LL NEVER WALK ALONE

ROBERT MARC JONES
Birthdate: 5 November 1971
Birthplace: Wrexham
Height: 5' 11"
Weight: 11st
Previous club: Crewe Alexandra
International Honours:
England Full, Under-21, Youth
Wales Schools

MACCA the CRACKER

Anfield favourite Steve McManaman was an almost permanent fixture in the Reds line-up during the 1997-98 campaign and, although he bagged double figures in goals, he will look back on the season with a tinge of disappointment. On a personal level Macca scored more times in '97-98 than during any other season since he made his debut in the early 90s. But at the end of it all there was nothing to show for so much endeavour.

Steve's season had started brightly enough with three goals coming before the end of September, contributing to victories over Leeds United and Aston Villa and a well-earned draw at Celtic in the first round of the UEFA Cup. That goal against Celtic was typical of Steve, a quite stunning finish following brilliant approach work.

A month after his wonderful solo strike against Villa, Steve scored in the 4-0 demolition of Derby, a rare header from a Stig Bjornebye corner-kick. More goals followed against Spurs and the eventual Champions, Arsenal, as the Reds won 1-0 at Highbury, courtesy of a cracker from Macca. It was the Gunners' first home defeat of the season.

Crystal Palace were the third London side to suffer at the hands of the **Liverpool** flyer as he got the ball rolling at Selhurst Park, the prelude to a 3-0 success. At the end of the year the Reds enjoyed a wonderful 2-1 win at Newcastle where Steve did his stuff once more, equalising a Steve Watson goal with an unstoppable volley into the roof of the net, then converting Michael Owen's cross before half-time.

In March he continued his good work against London opposition by bagging a brace against Spurs. He put on a five-star performance, tormenting the Tottenham rearguard with a series of tantalising runs. After poaching a first-half equaliser the Reds arrived at the final minute of the match 3-2 behind – until Macca struck to earn a thrilling draw.

Roy Evans said afterwards: "Steve was phenomenal. We gave him a slightly different role and he caused Tottenham all kinds of trouble, but then he always takes responsibility whether it's in attack or defence."

Steve broke Barnsley hearts in the Reds' next match at Oakwell, hitting the winner in stoppage time after the Tykes had equalised with five minutes left.

With a title challenge, the UEFA Cup and qualification for Euro 2000 to look forward to, the 1998-99 season is going to be a mouth-watering prospect for Steve McManaman, one of the truly great talents of English football.

Macca twists and turns against Barnsley

29

THE GERMAN

Karlheinz Riedle, the vastly experienced German international with more than 40 caps to his credit, was signed by the Reds in the summer of 1997. Karlheinz had just helped **BORUSSIA DORTMUND** to win the European Champions' Cup by scoring twice in the 3-1 victory over Juventus, and he initially thought he would be partnering Robbie Fowler up front at the outset of the 1997-98 campaign. But an injury to Robbie on a pre-season tour in Oslo enforced a new partnership, with Michael Owen.

Karlheinz played in Liverpool's first seven matches but when Robbie was fit to return, the German star was forced to play more of a substitute role rather than being an automatic first choice. After Robbie's unfortunate injury against Everton in February, Karlheinz found himself back in favour and he responded with two important strikes at Barnsley, plus valuable contributions in the victories over West Ham and Arsenal as the season drew to a close.

On the international front, Riedle has an impressive record. He played in the finals of the 1990 World Cup tournament and had scored a priceless goal against Holland at the qualification stages. He also took part in the 1994 tournament and that experience will be vital to the

Karlheinz leaps over Celtic's Stephane Mane

CONNECTION!

younger members of the **Liverpool** side as they make their own assault on the Premiership title this season.

Karlheinz will be hoping that **Liverpool**'s UEFA Cup adventure in 1998-99 has a happier ending than last season's exploits, which finished in such bitter disappointment in Strasbourg. He will also be hoping to hit the back of the net on a more regular basis and score the sort of goals that he's famous for – like the brilliant header he executed at Southampton last season and the controlled manner in which he finished a wonderful move at home to Aston Villa two days later.

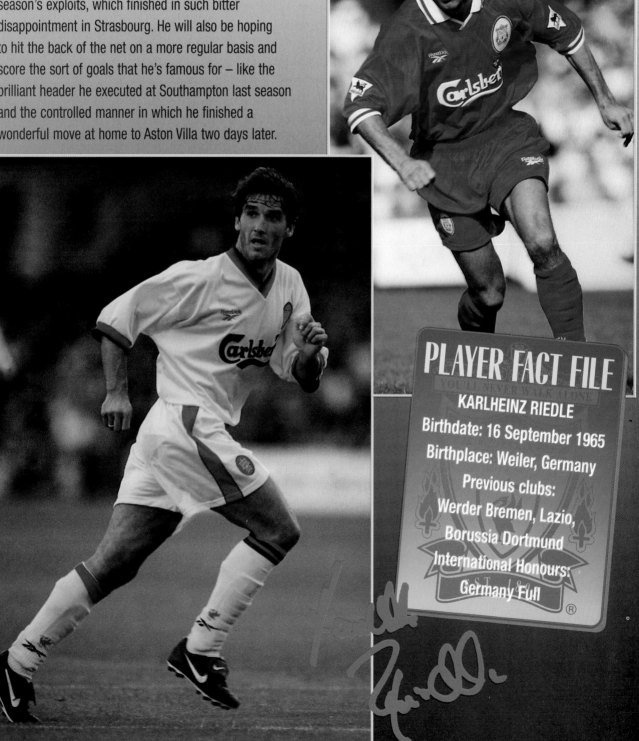

PLAYER FACT FILE

YOU'LL NEVER WALK ALONE

KARLHEINZ RIEDLE
Birthdate: 16 September 1965
Birthplace: Weiler, Germany
Previous clubs:
Werder Bremen, Lazio,
Borussia Dortmund
International Honours:
Germany Full

REDS
IN ACTION

Redknapp on the run versus Barnsley

Stretching for it – Paul Ince

A Liverpool trio refuses to go with the Flo!

Stig shows his determination against Wednesday

NORWAY KNOW-HOW

Norway supplies more players to the Premiership's 'Foreign Legion' than any other overseas country. Liverpool have three of the best...

34

OYVIND LEONHARDSEN

As a boy in his native Norway, Oyvind hero-worshipped Anfield aces Kenny Dalglish and Kevin Keegan and it was always his ambition to play for Liverpool. That dream was fulfilled in June 1997 when he made his move from **WIMBLEDON**. Unfortunately, Oyvind was unable to start the season because of an injury sustained in Ireland shortly before the Big Kick-off. At first it was estimated that he would be out for just a matter of weeks, but it turned out to be two and a half months!

When he did finally make his Liverpool baptism it was as a half-time substitute against West Bromwich Albion in the Third Round of the Coca-Cola Cup at The Hawthorns, which the Reds won 2-0. From then on there was no looking back and in his fourth appearance, at home to Derby County, he opened his goal-scoring account in an emphatic 4-0 victory.

"I was pleased with that goal," Oyvind said afterwards. "Firstly because it was important in the context of the match as it gave us a nice cushion of two goals, but also because I struck the ball well out of the reach of the goalkeeper." Oyvind went on to hit several more vital goals

PLAYER FACT FILE

YOU'LL NEVER WALK ALONE

OYVIND LEONHARDSEN

Birthdate: 17 August 1970

Birthplace: Norway

Height: 5' 10"

Weight: 11st 2lb

Previous club: Wimbledon

International Honours:

Norway Full

for the Reds and can be well satisfied with his first season at Anfield. He now looks forward to a successful Premiership season ahead and the added spice in the shape of the UEFA Cup. He will also be keen to add to his 60-plus internationals as Norway attempt to qualify for the European Championship finals in the year 2000.

NORWAY KNOW-HOW

PLAYER FACT FILE

STIG INGE BJORNEBYE

Birthdate: 11 December 1969
Birthplace: Elvcrum, Norway
Height: 5' 10"
Weight: 11st 9lb
Previous club: Rosenborg
International Honours:
Norway Full

STIG INGE BJORNEBYE

A Norwegian international signed by Graeme Souness from **ROSENBORG** in 1992 for £600,000, Stig is able to operate as an out-and-out defender, in a midfield role or in his more recent position of wing-back. He played in the Reds' first 22 games of the 1997-98 season, but lost his place in mid-season before returning towards the end of the campaign. Stig is his own biggest critic and, while he was happy with his contribution in '96-97, he was less than satisfied with his performances last season.

"I started the season slowly and struggled a bit in the early games," he said. "I wasn't playing anywhere near as well as I would have liked."

Things did improve though for the powerful Norwegian and he happily slotted into a wing-back role. "I like to think I'm flexible in a 4-4-2 or 3-5-2 system. The good thing is we have the players who can do jobs for the side other than those roles they would probably choose themselves."

It's going to be an important season ahead for Stig as he aims to help Liverpool achieve success in the UEFA Cup and to prise the Premiership trophy away from Arsenal. Added to that, there's the important personal matter of Norway's qualification for Euro 2000 and he'll be keen that they progress from a group that contains Greece, Georgia, Latvia, Slovenia and Albania.

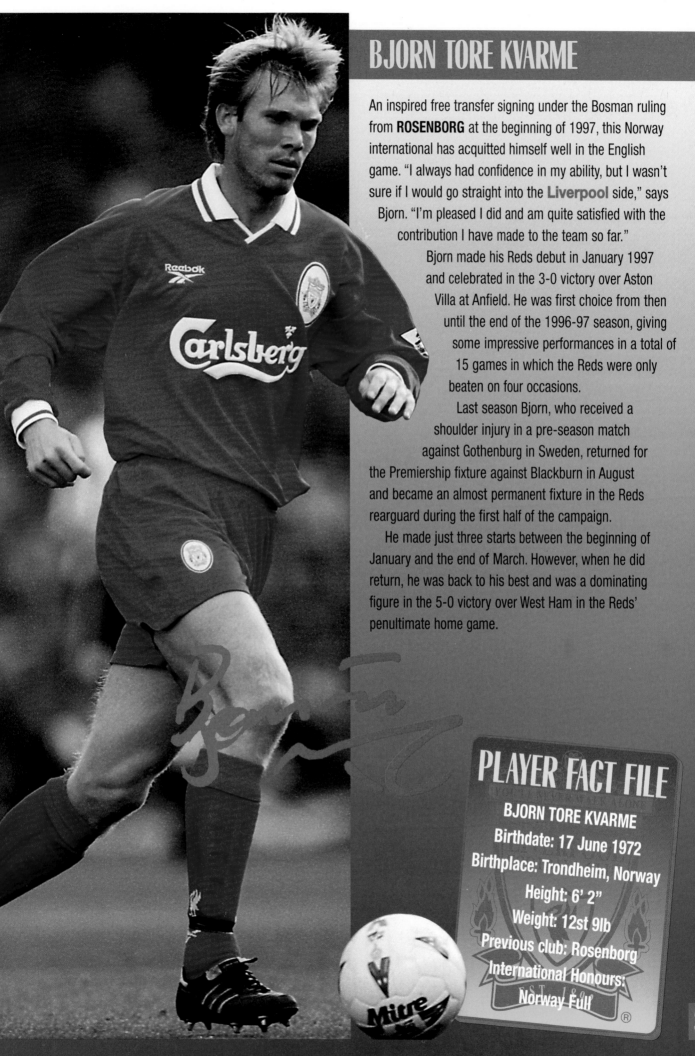

BJORN TORE KVARME

An inspired free transfer signing under the Bosman ruling from **ROSENBORG** at the beginning of 1997, this Norway international has acquitted himself well in the English game. "I always had confidence in my ability, but I wasn't sure if I would go straight into the **Liverpool** side," says Bjorn. "I'm pleased I did and am quite satisfied with the contribution I have made to the team so far."

Bjorn made his Reds debut in January 1997 and celebrated in the 3-0 victory over Aston Villa at Anfield. He was first choice from then until the end of the 1996-97 season, giving some impressive performances in a total of 15 games in which the Reds were only beaten on four occasions.

Last season Bjorn, who received a shoulder injury in a pre-season match against Gothenburg in Sweden, returned for the Premiership fixture against Blackburn in August and became an almost permanent fixture in the Reds rearguard during the first half of the campaign.

He made just three starts between the beginning of January and the end of March. However, when he did return, he was back to his best and was a dominating figure in the 5-0 victory over West Ham in the Reds' penultimate home game.

PLAYER FACT FILE

BJORN TORE KVARME
Birthdate: 17 June 1972
Birthplace: Trondheim, Norway
Height: 6' 2"
Weight: 12st 9lb
Previous club: Rosenborg
International Honours:
Norway Full

Phil came to prominence while playing for the Republic of Ireland in the 1994 World Cup finals in the United States. His self-assured performances in that tournament persuaded Liverpool to pay **COVENTRY CITY** £3.6 million for his services.

He started out as a trainee at **MILLWALL** in 1987, but left The Den to join former Millwall boss, John Docherty, at **BRADFORD CITY** during the 1990 close season. Phil scored on his League debut for the Bantams, coming on as a substitute against Reading in September 1990. In those days he operated as a left-back but, in February 1991, he suddenly appeared in the number nine shirt – as a striker! The change resulted in Phil finishing that season as Bradford's second highest goalscorer, with ten League goals. He continued up front in 1991-92, but was moved into the centre of defence by new manager Frank Stapleton. At the end of that season he moved to **COVENTRY CITY** for £500,000.

During 1997-98, injury punctuated Phil's season, which was a great pity after he had made such a promising start. His great pace is one of his chief assets and, according to Roy Evans, he was badly missed when absent at a critical time for the club. Phil's great positional sense and unflappable presence will be invaluable to the Reds as they make another tilt at the title.

PLAYER FACT FILE

YOU'LL NEVER WALK ALONE

PHILIP ANDREW BABB
Birthdate: 30 November 1970
Birthplace: Lambeth
Height: 6' 0"
Weight: 12st 3lb
Previous clubs: Millwall, Bradford City, Coventry City
International Honours: Republic of Ireland 'B' & Full

A former England youth and Under-21 international who has won four caps at intermediate level, Dominic has graduated through the ranks at Anfield, arriving initially at the club as an associated schoolboy in 1989 and becoming a trainee a year later.

He is now an integral part of the Reds back four, having made over 30 League appearances last season. One very encouraging sign was Dominic's inclusion in the England 'B' squad for the game against Chile at The Hawthorns last February.

"We were defeated on the night, but I enjoyed being involved," he said. His inclusion in the side showed that Glenn Hoddle had not erased the youngster from his thoughts following his elevation to the senior squad in 1997.

"Obviously my ambition is to get back into the full squad and I know that is going to be difficult, but it is certainly something I will be aiming for," says Big Dom.

Matteo has shown great adaptability, not only in the different systems that Liverpool have adopted of late, but in being able to play alongside a variety of defenders. It augers well for the future of the 24-year-old, whose calm, mature displays are sure to be a feature at Anfield for many seasons to come.

PLAYER FACT FILE

YOU'LL NEVER WALK ALONE

DOMINIC MATTEO
Birthdate: 24 April 1974
Birthplace: Dumfries
Height: 6' 1"
Weight: 11st 8lb
Previous clubs: None
International Honours:
England 'B', Under-21 & Youth

The 1997-98 season was one of disappointment for Liverpool's bubbly Republic of Ireland international. From the outset Jason was on the substitutes' bench, losing out to Rob Jones, whose place he had filled in the right wing-back role the previous campaign.

It was a job he had done admirably when the former England full-back was sidelined through injury. But those roles were to be reversed at the start of the 1997-98 season. Jason made just four starts between early August and late November, but his patience was rewarded in the weeks leading up to Christmas when he found himself back in favour.

Then disaster struck. In January, following a 14 match run in the first team, he broke his leg against Blackburn Rovers. He was absent for three months, but returned to face West Ham in early May. Liverpool won 5-0 and the match was a personal triumph for Jason, who gave an inspired performance and scored twice.

A Liverpool fan through and through, it was a dream come true when he arrived at Anfield from **BOLTON WANDERERS** in 1995. "I only want to play for Liverpool," he has said. That's a tribute to him, despite plenty of transfer speculation following his omission a year ago. Many players would have wanted to get away, but Jason was always optimistic that if he worked hard enough he would get a recall. Let's hope his injury worries are a thing of the past and he helps his favourites to major honours this term.

PLAYER FACT FILE

JASON WYNN McATEER
Birthdate: 18 June 1971
Birthplace: Birkenhead
Height: 5' 11"
Weight: 11st 5lb
Previous club:
Bolton Wanderers
International Honours:
Republic of Ireland 'B' & Full

Jason is challenged by Man United's Andy Cole

Inset: Jason suffers the agony of a broken leg in the match against Blackburn

ANFIELD'S
GUV'NOR

Signed from **INTER MILAN** before the start of last season, Paul Ince is the first to acknowledge that the past campaign was a great disappointment for himself and the club. "We have the ability, but we were careless with some of the points we dropped," he said. "Lessons have been learned which will hopefully stand us in good stead for the next campaign."

While he enjoyed his first season at Anfield, Paul put Liverpool's failure to land a trophy down to inconsistency. "There were times when some of the football we played was first class and it was a pleasure to be involved. But there were other games when we didn't do ourselves justice."

On a personal level, he enjoyed a virtually injury-free season, although no-one in England will forget the bloodied forehead, swathed in a white bandage, that accompanied England's triumphant World Cup qualification with that never-to-be-forgotten 0-0 draw in Italy in October 1997.

Ince, made captain for the night in the absence of Alan Shearer, was a true general, marshalling his troops in impressive fashion. After the match he said: "I have never been so nervous before a game. It didn't have anything to do with being captain. I think I just realised that it was probably my last chance of going to the World Cup."

Now Paul will be looking forward to leading the charge towards Euro 2000, as England prepare for Bulgaria, Luxembourg, Poland and Sweden in Group Five of the qualifying tournament.

Back on the domestic front, Paul is not a person who accepts second best, so you can expect him to be giving his all as Liverpool attempt to win their first title since 1990. He'll want to hit the double figures mark in terms of goals too – something he missed out on in 1997-98. He

41

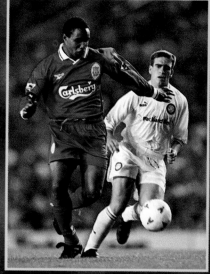

Inset: Liverpool's skipper
in action against Leeds

42

ANFIELD'S
GUV'NOR

made a good enough start, scoring against Leicester in only his second match, and he followed that up with a goal versus Sheffield Wednesday three games later. But then he didn't add to his tally until February, when he scored in the one-all draw with Everton.

In March, he found the net in successive matches against Bolton and Tottenham, then scored against his former club **WEST HAM UNITED**, before hitting a brace in the memorable 4-0 win over newly crowned Champions Arsenal.

It was at West Ham, of course, where Paul began his career as a 14-year-old associated schoolboy in December 1981, graduating through the Youth Training Scheme. He signed professional forms for the Hammers in 1985 and made his Football League debut a year later, coming on as a substitute at Newcastle United. He kept his place a week later, to play in his first full game, against Southampton at Upton Park. The Hammers won 3-1 and Paul scored the opening goal on his home debut.

In 1989, after 72 League appearances, he was sold to **MANCHESTER UNITED** for £1.25 million. The following year, he won an FA Cup winners' medal as United beat Crystal Palace. In 1991, he helped United lift the European Cup Winners' Cup following victory over Barcelona. A year on he enjoyed League Cup success at Wembley as United beat Forest. He also made his England debut against Spain.

In 1993 and 1994 United won back-to-back Premiership titles and Paul won an FA Cup Winners' medal following a 4-0 triumph over Chelsea. In 1995, he was signed by **INTER MILAN** for £7 million, which is still the record transfer fee received by Manchester United.

Now he is an Anfield-ite through and through and his dearest ambition is to help add a few more trophies to Liverpool's impressive Roll of Honour.

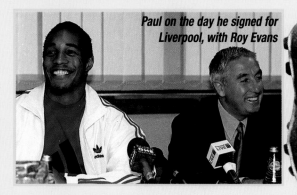

Paul on the day he signed for Liverpool, with Roy Evans

43

Steve Harkness signed for the Reds from his local side **CARLISLE UNITED** in July 1989 and, after spending much of his Anfield career covering for injured defenders, he would be the first to agree that last season was his best in terms of first team appearances.

He played in the first five games of the campaign, but then an untimely injury put paid to any long term continuity. However, Steve kept working hard in training and was recalled for the UEFA Cup-tie in Strasbourg. Unfortunately, the whole side gave a below-par performance and Steve was one of the casualties. He then spent the next eight games on the substitutes' bench without being called upon. But he bided his time and earned a recall for the away game against Crystal Palace. The Reds won 3-0 and Steve didn't look back, keeping his place right through to the end of the season.

PLAYER FACT FILE

STEVEN HARKNESS
Birthdate: 27 August 1971
Birthplace: Carlisle
Height: 5' 10"
Weight: 11st 2lb
Previous clubs: Carlisle United,
Huddersfield Town (loan),
Southend United (loan)

Jamie Carragher won't forget his debut in a Liverpool shirt, a substitute appearance against West Ham at Anfield in January 1997. He did enough to keep his place for the next home game versus Aston Villa and scored the first goal in a memorable 3-0 victory. It wasn't just the goal that earned him rave reviews, but his overall performance which showed great maturity.

Jamie was selected for the England Under-20 side that took part in the World Youth Championships in the summer of 1997. He helped the side win their three group matches against the Ivory Coast, the United Arab Emirates and Mexico. In the next round, the Youth side met Argentina and lost 2-1, with Jamie scoring the England goal. "They were a really good side and went on to win the competition," he said.

When Liverpool's 1997-98 campaign began, Jamie found himself involved in the second game against Leicester, coming on as a second half substitute. Thereafter, he had his best season in terms of first team appearances, ending up with over 20 including three as substitute. He had some fine games in the red shirt too, none more so than in the local derby at home to Everton in February, when many considered him to be Liverpool's Man of the Match.

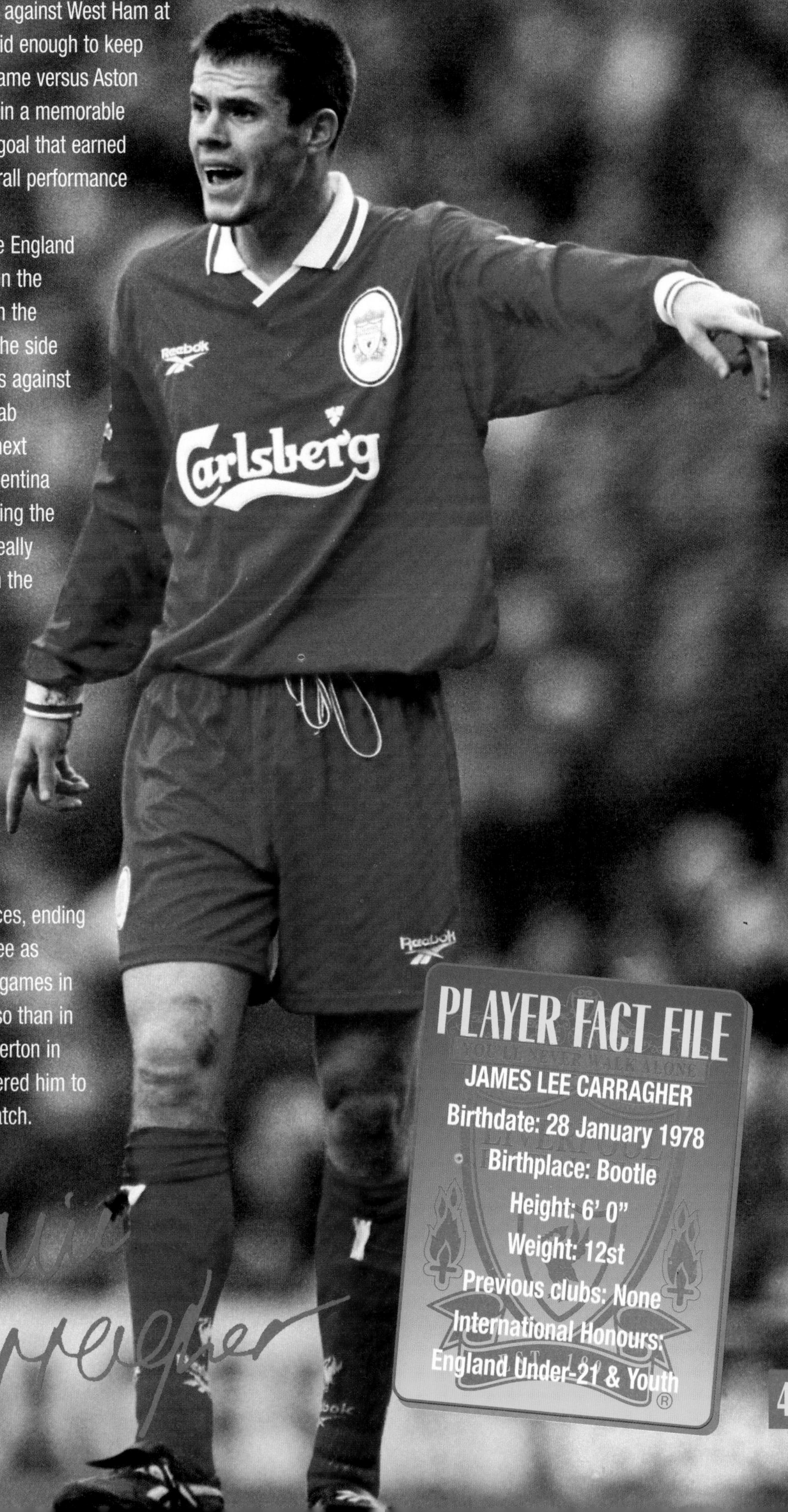

PLAYER FACT FILE

JAMES LEE CARRAGHER
Birthdate: 28 January 1978
Birthplace: Bootle
Height: 6' 0"
Weight: 12st
Previous clubs: None
International Honours: England Under-21 & Youth

45

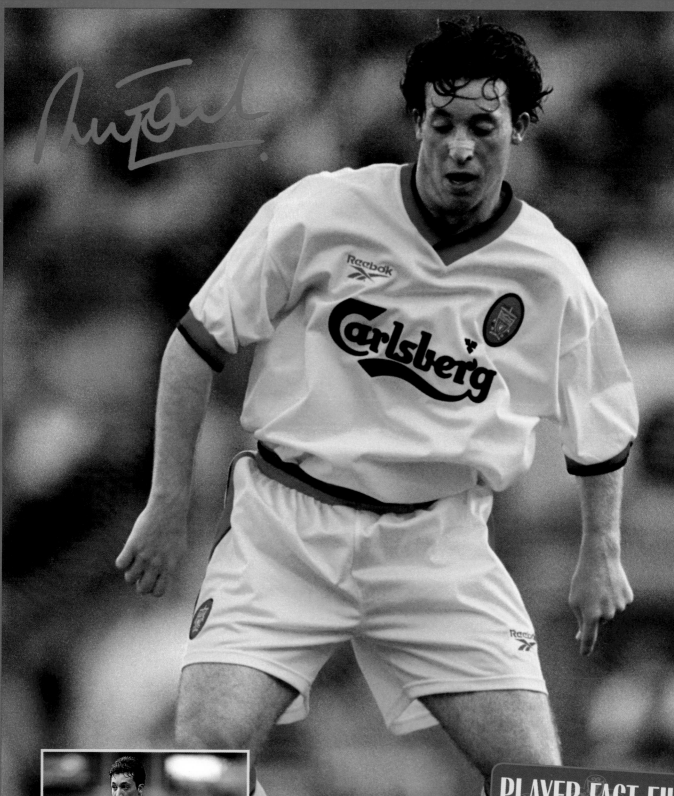

PLAYER FACT FILE
YOU'LL NEVER WALK ALONE

ROBERT BERNARD FOWLER

Birthdate: 9 April 1975

Birthplace: Liverpool

Height: 5' 11"

Weight: 11st 10lb

Previous clubs: None

International Honours:

England Full, 'B', Under-21 & Youth

EST 1892 ®

ROBBED!
OF A PLACE IN FRANCE

Named as the PFA's Young Player of the Year in 1995 and again in 1996, Robbie is a product of **Liverpool**'s School of Excellence. And he has excelled ever since he pulled on the famous red shirt for the first time in 1993.

Robbie missed the opening six games of the 1997-98 season through an injury picked up after he had scored twice in a pre-season friendly in Oslo. But in his first full appearance, at home to Aston Villa, he was back with a bang and scored from the spot. He then hit three in four games, against West Ham and Chelsea in the Premiership and against West Brom in the 3rd Round of the Coca-Cola Cup. Ten days after the Baggies match, Derby were on the receiving end of a 'Robbie Roasting' – he scored twice as **Liverpool** slipped into overdrive and cruised home 4-0.

Goals against Bolton and Strasbourg followed in the Reds next two matches and Robbie would have been flying – if not for the fact that he got himself sent off against the Wanderers and missed three important games. When he

did return to action, against Manchester United, he scored from the spot, but it was not enough to stop United who hit three of their own.

On Boxing Day Robbie hit the target twice in the 3-1 win over Leeds, then scored important Coca-Cola Cup goals against Newcastle and Middlesbrough before his season was curtailed by a serious knee ligament injury in the derby against Everton on 23 February.

On the England front, Robbie collected his seventh cap, against Cameroon at Wembley in November 1997, and got on the score sheet as England won 2-0. World Cup selection would probably have been a formality for Fowler, but the knee injury prevented him being included in Glenn Hoddle's final 22 for France. Now Robbie will be looking to return to top form this season as England begin their quest to qualify for the European Championship finals, to be staged jointly by Belgium and Holland in the year 2000. Everyone at **Liverpool** FC wishes him well in his recovery.

Happy and unhappy times for Robbie Fowler

PLAYER FACT FILE
YOU'LL NEVER WALK ALONE

JAMIE FRANK REDKNAPP
Birthdate: 25 June 1973
Birthplace: Barton-on-Sea
Height: 5' 11"
Weight: 11st 8lbs
Previous club: Bournemouth
International Honours:
England Full, 'B' & Under-21

JAMIE JUST KEEPS ON COMING BACK

Just when he thought he had seen the back of injuries that disrupted the 1995-96 and 1996-97 seasons, Jamie Redknapp suffered a serious ankle injury while playing for England against South Africa in May 1997.

It was all the more galling for the talented midfielder because he suffered a similar fate against Scotland during Euro '96. In only his third international outing, against Switzerland, he tore a hamstring and was out for the next three months, so it's no wonder he feels he is due a change of fortune. "People keep pointing out to me that all my injuries seem to occur when I'm playing for England,"

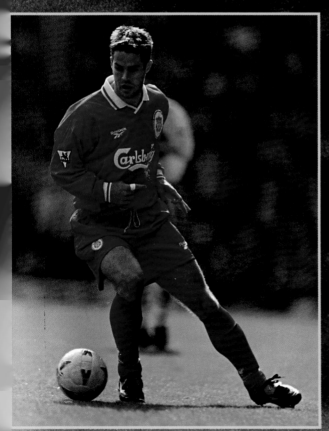

he says. "But it's just a succession of coincidences really."

The injury against South Africa was particularly untimely, especially as it occurred just before England's summer tournament in France, which would have been the perfect opportunity for Jamie to relaunch his international career. "I was beginning to get back to my best form and was looking forward to a sustained run in the England side."

Instead, it meant him missing **Liverpool**'s first 13 games of last season, but when he did return it was for the fateful 3-0 defeat by Strasbourg in the 2nd Round of the UEFA Cup. It was scant consolation that Jamie was named **Liverpool**'s Man of the Match.

In his fifth game, he scored the third goal in the Reds' 4-0 romp against Tottenham at Anfield, hammering home a great right foot shot following a pass from Robbie Fowler.

Jamie began 1998 with a goal in the FA Cup 3rd Round at home to Coventry, but the Sky Blues hit back with three of their own. He went one better the following week against Wimbledon, scoring two crackers to earn top billing for the second home match running.

Just when Jamie thought the bad luck was behind him, the injury jinx struck again, only days before the England squad was due to be announced for the Chile friendly at Wembley last February. He had just scored for the Reds against Middlesbrough in the 1st Leg of the Coca-Cola Cup semi-final, helping them to a 2-1 home success, when he fell victim to a damaged cartilage. It kept him out for five matches but he returned for the home derby against Everton. Then, after six appearances in March and April, he received a further injury which subsequently eliminated him from selection for England's World Cup squad.

JANUARY 1998

On 3 January **Liverpool** welcomed **COVENTRY CITY** back to Anfield, having beaten them 1-0 in the Premiership two weeks earlier. This time the prize at stake was a place in the 4th Round of the FA Cup. Roy Evans was quick to remind the fans that the Premiership match would have no bearing on the cup-tie; this would be a different game altogether – and so it proved to be!

Even though **Liverpool** struck first with a well-taken free-kick by Jamie Redknapp, Coventry took command of the game. The Sky Blues strike force of Darren Huckerby and Dion Dublin were in inspirational form. They both scored, as did Paul Telfer, for a 3-1 victory.

Having been unceremoniously dumped out of the FA Cup, **Liverpool**'s next match would determine their fate in the Coca-Cola competition. After the successes against West Brom and Grimsby, the Reds now faced their toughest test in the tournament – a visit to **NEWCASTLE UNITED** in the 5th Round on 7 January.

After 90 minutes both sides had had numerous opportunities to take the lead, but the scoreline stood at 0-0 and the game slipped into extra time. It was Michael Owen who eventually broke the deadlock in the 95th minute when he outpaced Aaron Hughes to meet a wonderful through ball from Robbie Fowler. Michael then chipped the ball over Shaka Hislop and into the net.

Robbie Fowler was the on-target man for **Liverpool**'s second. It came in the 103rd minute. This time the through ball came from Oyvind Leonhardsen. Robbie met it perfectly and slotted home from eight yards out. The 2-0 scoreline took the Reds into the two-legged semi-final encounter with Bryan Robson's Middlesbrough.

It was back to Premiership action on 10 January, with **WIMBLEDON**'s visit to Anfield. The Dons had become something of a 'bogey' team to **Liverpool** in recent encounters. In fact, the last time the Reds had recorded a League victory over Wimbledon was in the 1994-95 season. That trend was halted by a decisive **Liverpool** performance – a 2-0 victory in which Jamie Redknapp bagged both goals late in the game. The first, on 72 minutes, came from a defence-splitting through ball from Steve McManaman. Jamie was quick to react and his shot beat Neil Sullivan in the Dons goal. Jamie's second came in the 84th minute after he collected a short pass from Michael Owen and fired home from all of 20 yards.

Seven days later **Liverpool** travelled to *Filbert Street*, home of **LEICESTER CITY**. The match ended in the Reds' second 0-0 draw of the season so far. It was a dour encounter with **Liverpool** doing most of the attacking and coming up against a solid Leicester defence that gave nothing away.

On Tuesday 20 January **Liverpool** met **NEWCASTLE UNITED** for the third time in three weeks. This meeting was the Premiership fixture at Anfield. On the previous evening Southampton had beaten runaway table-toppers Manchester United 1-0 at *The Dell*, a result that gave renewed hope to the chasing pack of Blackburn, Chelsea, **Liverpool** and Arsenal. Thanks to a Michael Owen goal in

1997-98 part two

... CONTINUED FROM PAGE 20

the 17th minute – made by a superb tackle on Jon Dahl Tomasson by Paul Ince and a pass by Jason McAteer – the Reds beat the Magpies 1-0. The result took **Liverpool** to third place in the table, their highest position of the season so far.

First Division **MIDDLESBROUGH** were Anfield's next visitors, on 27 January, for the 1st leg of the Coca-Cola Cup semi-final. Wembley's twin towers began to loom enticingly on the horizon when goals from Jamie Redknapp (a 30-yard special) and Robbie Fowler (a right-foot thunderbolt) ensured victory for the home side. Paul Merson had opened the scoring for 'Boro, in a 2-1 result that set up a fascinating return leg three weeks later.

Liverpool's final fixture of January 1998 brought Roy Hodgson's **BLACKBURN ROVERS** to Anfield in the Premiership. It also produced a 0-0 draw between the two

RED FACT

Robbie Fowler's goal against Middlesbrough in the Coca-Cola Cup semi-final 1st leg was his 20th in that competition. It was in the Coca-Cola Cup that hot-shot Robbie first hit the headlines when he scored all five goals in Liverpool's 5-0 2nd leg victory against Fulham in 1993.

"Ouch!" says Leicester's Neil Lennon as Incey goes for the ball!

Michael is blocked by Leicester's Matt Elliot

Michael Owen celebrates his winner against Newcastle

51

THE REDS IN 1997-98

sides who were then both following Manchester United at the top of the table. The division of the points helped neither side as Chelsea won 2-0 at Barnsley to leapfrog into second spot. At the same time, leaders Manchester United were losing 1-0 to Leicester City and the gap at the top was slowly but surely closing. Another ominous result down in London saw Arsenal beating Southampton 3-0. This was the start of a championship challenge revival that would ultimately take the Gunners all the way.

Jamie gets airborne against Newcastle

Michael in action against Blackburn

RESULT	COMPETITION	DATE	STADIUM	ATTENDANCE
Liverpool 1, Coventry 3	FA Cup (3)	3.1.98	Anfield	33,888
Newcastle 0, Liverpool 2	Coca-Cola Cup (5)	7.1.98	St James' Park	33,207
Liverpool 2, Wimbledon 0	Premiership	10.1.98	Anfield	38,011
Leicester City 0, Liverpool 0	Premiership	17.1.98	Filbert Street	21,633
Liverpool 1, Newcastle 0	Premiership	20.1.98	Anfield	42,791
Liverpool 2, Middlesbrough 1	Coca-Cola Cup (sf)	27.1.98	Anfield	33,438
Liverpool 0, Blackburn 0	Premiership	31.1.98	Anfield	43,890

January '98

FEBRUARY 1998

On 7 February **SOUTHAMPTON** came to Anfield, grabbed all three points and put a big dent in **Liverpool**'s title ambitions. The Saints struck the first blow with a David Hirst penalty after only eight minutes. But the Reds got back into it 16 minutes later when Michael Owen hammered the ball into the roof of the visitors' net.

After that it became a real battle and it was the Saints who edged ahead through Egil Ostenstadt in the 85th minute. Then in the 89th minute David Hirst made it 3-1 to the visitors. Michael Owen pulled one back for the Reds with a header in the dying seconds of the game. But, of course, it just wasn't enough.

There was no love lost on **Liverpool**'s trip to **SHEFFIELD WEDNESDAY** on St Valentine's Day. Wednesday opened the scoring in the 7th minute when Benito Carbone lobbed the ball over David James. Twenty minutes later Michael Owen's pace earned the Reds an equaliser – he outran Jon Newsome to latch on to Steve McManaman's through ball which he then slotted home.

In the space of six minutes in the second half, Wednesday appeared to take the initiative with goals from Paulo Di Canio and Andy Hinchcliffe. The home side must have thought the three points were safe and sound. If so, they had reckoned without Michael Owen.

Three days earlier Michael had made that historic international debut for England against Chile at Wembley. Now, at Hillsborough, he was about to advance his reputation even further. In the 73rd minute Robbie Fowler hammered a shot that rebounded off the post. Michael was on hand to slot it home. Five minutes later he produced another great shot to fire the Reds equaliser and salvage a

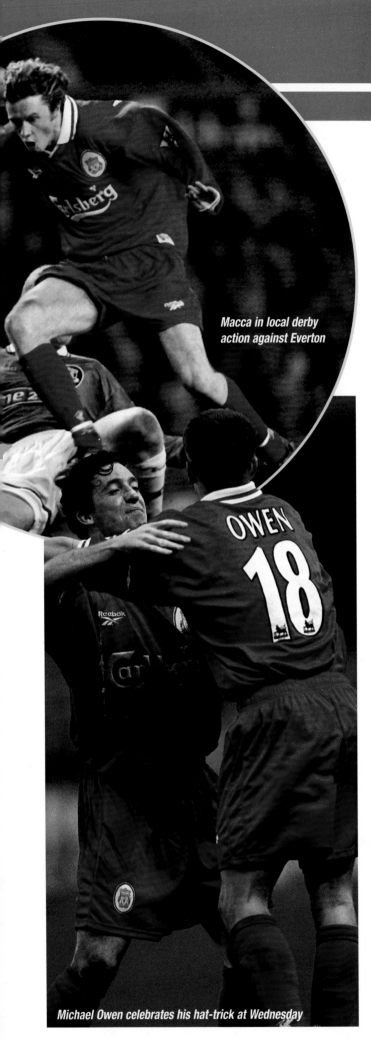

Macca in local derby action against Everton

Michael Owen celebrates his hat-trick at Wednesday

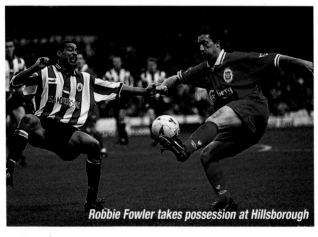

Robbie Fowler takes possession at Hillsborough

Jamie Carragher gets to the ball first at Villa Park

54

RESULT	COMPETITION	DATE	STADIUM	ATTENDANCE
Liverpool 2, Southampton 3	Premiership	7.2.98	Anfield	43,550
Sheffield Wed 3, Liverpool 3	Premiership	14.2.98	Hillsborough	35,405
Middlesbrough 2, Liverpool 0	Coca-Cola Cup (sf)	18.2.98	Riverside	29,828
Liverpool 1, Everton 1	Premiership	23.2.98	Anfield	44,501
Aston Villa 2, Liverpool 1	Premiership	28.2.98	Villa Park	39,372

much needed point. It was a performance that had Roy Evans and the Liverpool fans singing the young lad's praises. The single point was enough to leapfrog Liverpool into second place in the Premiership table, behind Manchester United.

Four days later Liverpool travelled to **MIDDLESBROUGH** for the 2nd Leg of the Coca-Cola Cup semi-final. Things began to go wrong right from the start when Jamie Carragher fouled Mikkel Beck in the area and Boro's Paul Merson made no mistake from the spot.

Then to compound Liverpool's woes, Boro's brand new Italian star Marco Branca put the home side two-up in the 4th minute. Later Roy Evans would describe Liverpool's dire display in this period of the game as 'kamikaze football'. The 2-0 scoreline meant, of course, that Boro were now 3-2 ahead on aggregate. From then on they defended well to prevent Liverpool from scoring – and to knock them out of the competition. Middlesbrough went on to lose to Chelsea in the Coca-Cola Cup final at Wembley.

But Liverpool were still left with a tilt at the biggest prize of them all, the FA Premier League trophy. At this stage in the competition Roy Evans' side were still in with a chance of success. And, of course, second place would ensure qualification for the European Champions League, while any top six finish would give the club another crack at the UEFA Cup in 1998-99 – so there was still everything to play for.

The next obstacle in Liverpool's title challenge was the visit to Anfield on 23 February of local rivals **EVERTON**, who were still fighting to stay out of the relegation zone. The Blues scored first through big Duncan Ferguson in the 58th minute. Eight minutes later Liverpool equalised when Paul Ince fired home Michael Owen's cross. There were no more goals and the match ended all-square at 1-1. However, neither side gave up trying and, as the game

drew towards its end, Robbie Fowler bravely attempted to head home the winner. Unfortunately he was badly injured in the challenge. Later, in hospital, it was confirmed that Robbie had damaged knee ligaments – he would be absent not only for the remainder of the season, but was also ruled out of the reckoning for a place in England's World Cup finals squad. It was a bitter blow.

February closed with more depressing news for Liverpool, namely a defeat by **ASTON VILLA** at *Villa Park* on the 28th. Villa had recently parted company with manager Brian Little, and this was John Gregory's first game in charge. The visitors were on the receiving end of a Villa backlash in which ex-Anfielder Stan Collymore scored twice in what was probably his best performance of the season. Michael Owen had opened the scoring from the penalty spot in the 5th minute after Oyvind Leonhardsen had been brought down. Liverpool's performance was described by Roy Evans as 'average and disappointing'.

It had certainly done nothing whatsoever to enhance those Anfield ambitions and February ended with Liverpool slipping to 4th place in the Premiership table.

MARCH 1998

Things picked up again as the season moved into March, with a 2-1 victory over relegation battlers **BOLTON WANDERERS** at Anfield on the 7th. Bolton opened the scoring in the 7th minute when Alan Thompson finished off a neat move with Nathan Blake and they held onto the lead until early in the second half. Then the tables began to turn when Paul Ince equalised with a powerful header from substitute Mark Kennedy's corner-kick.

In the 65th minute Paul Ince turned provider when he slipped the ball to Michael Owen who finished with a touch of pure class to put the ball beyond Keith

THE REDS IN 1997-98

Paul Ince heads Liverpool's opener against Bolton

Branagan in the Bolton goal. The result lifted the Reds back into second position.

Next came three away fixtures in a row. The first was at *White Hart Lane*, home of **TOTTENHAM HOTSPUR** – a club still desperate for points at the wrong end of the table – and they almost took all three in what proved a thoroughly entertaining spectacle.

Jürgen Klinsmann, recently recalled to the fold to help Spurs through a difficult patch, was the first name on the score sheet when he headed home a David Ginola cross. Steve McManaman equalised for Liverpool eight minutes later after collecting Michael Owen's pass, surging into the Spurs penalty area and unleashing a deadly shot from 12 yards. Shortly after half time David Ginola, playing the game of his life, put Spurs ahead again with a remarkable shot from 20 yards out. Next it was Paul Ince's turn to equalise with a spectacular close range bicycle kick in the 63rd minute. In the 80th minute Ramon Vega headed Spurs back into the lead from a pinpoint cross delivered by David Ginola.

With two minutes left, time was running out for Liverpool. Then Michael Owen fired the ball against the

Karlheinz Riedle has just scored against Barnsley at Oakwell

Oyvind Leonhardsen outpaces the Spurs defence

post. It rebounded into the path of Steve McManaman who made no mistake in netting **Liverpool**'s third equaliser of the afternoon. It had been a great game and a great advertisement for English Premier League football.

Liverpool met struggling **BARNSLEY** at *Oakwell* on 28 March, hoping to avenge the 1-0 defeat suffered at Anfield back in November. Barnsley scored first through Neil Redfearn in the 37th minute. Karlheinz Riedle, making a comeback from injury, equalised for **Liverpool** by stabbing home a loose ball just before half time.

In the 59th minute Karlheinz scored again with an amazing shot from 35 yards. But Barnsley were by no means through. In the 85th minute Neil Redfearn got his second goal of the game, from the penalty spot, after Phil Babb fouled Georgi Hristov.

Liverpool's winner came in the last minute, when Paul Ince backheeled the ball into the path of Steve McManaman. Steve then jinked his way forward before lofting his shot over 'keeper David Watson into the net.

March had produced seven points for **Liverpool** out of a possible nine and the club ended the month at 3rd place in the Premiership table. Arsenal had now moved up into second position and Manchester United were leading the race by six points.

Dominic Matteo in action in the away win over Barnsley

MATCH FAX	RESULT	COMPETITION	DATE	STADIUM	ATTENDANCE	March '98
	Liverpool 2, Bolton 1	Premiership	7.3.98	Anfield	44,532	
	Tottenham 3, Liverpool 3	Premiership	14.3.98	White Hart Lane	30,245	
	Barnsley 2, Liverpool 3	Premiership	28.3.98	Oakwell	18,648	

THE REDS IN 1997-98

Macca goes past Manchester United's Nicky Butt

APRIL 1998

Having played against relegation candidates in their last three games, Liverpool now faced up to Premier League leaders **MANCHESTER UNITED** at Old Trafford on Good Friday, 10 April. Once again there was a point to prove, as United had won the corresponding fixture at Anfield back in December. As in that previous match United scored first – this time through Ronny Johnsen who headed home a David Beckham corner-kick in the 12th minute.

Twenty-four minutes later hot-shot Michael Owen took advantage of a moment of indecision in the United defence to fire home the equaliser. Later in the first half Michael would receive his marching orders from referee Poll, following a second bookable offence. The scoreline remained at 1-1 and gave Arsenal the opportunity to close the gap at the top of the table by beating Newcastle on the following day – which they duly did.

On Easter Monday, bottom club **CRYSTAL PALACE** came to Anfield in a desperate search for points. Liverpool took an early lead through Oyvind Leonhardsen, but late in the game Palace equalised when Marcus Bent lobbed 'keeper Brad Friedel. The Reds hero turned out to be young David Thompson who came on as a sub for Danny Murphy in the 70th minute – and then scored the winner from a Steve McManaman cross on 85 minutes.

Next came a trip to **COVENTRY CITY**'s *Highfield Road* on 18 April. In the 33rd minute Michael Owen notched his 21st goal of the season and he did it in spectacular fashion, latching on to a header from Stig Bjornebye, completely bamboozling defender Gary Breen and then belting the ball beyond 'keeper Steve Ogrizovic.

City equalised through Dion Dublin who scored from the penalty spot after Phil Babb was adjudged to have fouled Darren Huckerby. Liverpool then had a penalty claim denied and almost snatched victory when Karlheinz Riedle's shot went wide in the closing minutes.

Liverpool's last game in April was at *Stamford Bridge* in West London, where

Michael Owen – delighted with the equaliser against Manchester United

THE REDS IN 1997-98

they received a 4-1 drubbing from Coca-Cola Cup winners **CHELSEA**. The Reds' goal came from Karlheinz Riedle, but it was scant consolation and the team deserved their lengthy lecture from team boss Roy Evans. Even though the Premiership cause was effectively lost, there was still a UEFA Cup placing to confirm.

Top Left: Leonhardsen challenges Palace 'keeper Kevin Miller
Bottom left: Paul Ince cuts through the Chelsea defence
– but it was a day when the Reds got the Blues!
Above: David Thompson scores the winner against Crystal Palace
Below: Jamie Redknapp shields the ball from Willie Boland

MATCH FAX

RESULT	COMPETITION	DATE	STADIUM	ATTENDANCE
Man United 1, Liverpool 1	Premiership	10.4.98	Old Trafford	55,171
Liverpool 2, Crystal Palace 1	Premiership	13.4.98	Anfield	43,007
Coventry 1, Liverpool 1	Premiership	18.4.98	Highfield Road	22,721
Chelsea 4, Liverpool 1	Premiership	25.4.98	Stamford Bridge	34,639

April '98

MAY 1998

The lecture and the hard-earned lesson were taken to heart and in the next fixture against **WEST HAM UNITED** at Anfield on 2 May, **Liverpool** were a team transformed. By half time the Reds were 4-0 ahead, thanks to goals from Michael Owen, Oyvind Leonhardsen and Jason McAteer who scored twice. In the second half skipper Paul Ince smashed home a great 30 yard goal, to hammer home this defeat of the club where he had begun his career. The result assured **Liverpool** of European football in the 1998-99 UEFA Cup competition.

When **ARSENAL** came to Anfield on 6 May, they were already crowned as Premiership champions following an awesome display against Everton three days earlier. They were also looking ahead to the FA Cup final against Newcastle, in which a Gunners victory would clinch the much coveted 'double'. The Gunners may have had other things on

Macca and Arsenal's Lee Dixon go up for the ball

their minds, but **Liverpool** were in top form and determined to give the Anfield faithful a proper show in the last home game of the season. Two goals from Paul Ince and one each from Michael Owen and Oyvind Leonhardsen produced a convincing 4-0 scoreline. This result made **Liverpool** the only team to do the League double over Arsenal all season. It also confirmed that the Reds would finish third in the Premiership.

Liverpool's final match of the season took place at **DERBY COUNTY**'s *Pride Park*. Derby were still in with a chance of UEFA Cup qualification and they took charge against a reshuffled **Liverpool** line-up that was missing several first team regulars. The game was settled by a single goal from County's Paulo Wanchope. But Euro qualification eluded County, as other results went against them.

The season was all done. Yet, as always with **Liverpool** FC, there was feeling of disappointment that no major trophy had found its way to Anfield.

Roy Evans summed up the feelings of everyone involved with the club when he said: "This is the highest we have

Paul Ince scores...and celebrates Liverpool's fifth goal against the Hammers

finished for quite a long period and to finish third and get into Europe is no mean achievement. The only difference is the history of **Liverpool** Football Club."

Being called 'the nearly men' hurts a lot for everyone involved at Anfield. The club has a lot to prove in 1998-99 and that will make for another entertaining season at Anfield and all around the country as **Liverpool** FC strive to continue their long and proud tradition of winning trophies.

1997-98 — FA PREMIER LEAGUE — FINAL TABLE

	P	W	D	L	F	A	Pts
Arsenal	38	23	9	6	68	33	78
Manchester United	38	23	8	7	73	26	77
LIVERPOOL	38	18	11	9	68	42	65
Chelsea	38	20	3	15	71	43	63
Leeds United	38	17	8	13	57	46	59
Blackburn Rovers	38	16	10	12	57	52	58
Aston Villa	38	17	6	15	49	48	57
West Ham United	38	16	8	14	56	57	56
Derby County	38	16	7	15	52	49	55
Leicester City	38	13	14	11	51	41	53
Coventry City	38	12	16	10	46	44	52
Southampton	38	14	6	18	50	55	48
Newcastle United	38	11	11	16	35	44	44
Tottenham Hotspur	38	11	11	16	44	56	44
Wimbledon	38	10	14	14	34	46	44
Sheffield Wednesday	38	12	8	18	52	67	44
Everton	38	9	13	16	41	56	40
Bolton Wanderers	38	9	13	16	41	61	40
Barnsley	38	10	5	23	37	82	35
Crystal Palace	38	8	9	21	37	71	33

Michael Owen's spectacular strike against Champions Arsenal at Anfield

Jason McAteer celebrates with Michael Owen after scoring the third goal in the match with West Ham

LIVERPOOL GOALSCORERS 1997-98
(in all competitions)

Michael Owen	23
Robbie Fowler	13
Steve McManaman	12
Paul Ince	8
Karlheinz Riedle	7
Oyvind Leonhardsen	6
Jamie Redknapp	5
Patrik Berger	4
Jason McAteer	2
Michael Thomas	1
David Thompson	1

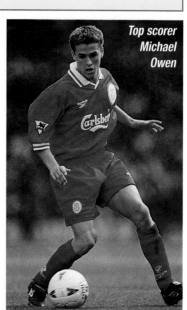

Top scorer Michael Owen

MATCH FAX

RESULT	COMPETITION	DATE	STADIUM	ATTENDANCE
Liverpool 5, West Ham United 0	Premiership	2.5.98	Anfield	44,414
Liverpool 4, Arsenal 0	Premiership	6.5.98	Anfield	44,417
Derby 1, Liverpool 0	Premiership	10.5.98	Pride Park	30,492

May '98